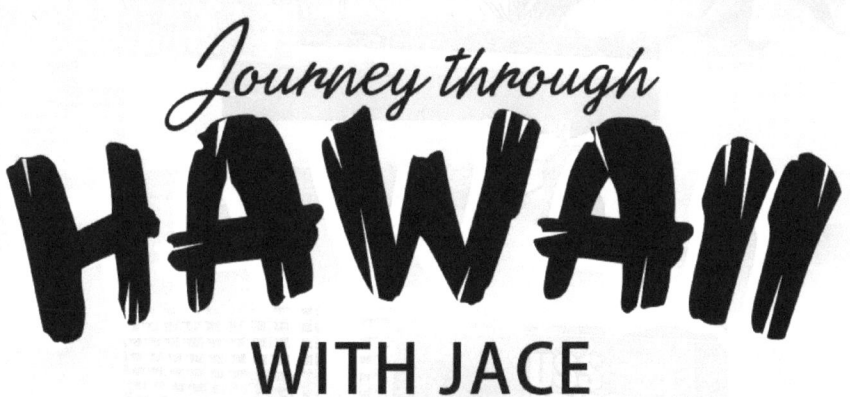

Journey through HAWAII
WITH JACE

JACE FENNELL

FENNELL ADVENTURES

Journey Through Hawaii with Jace
Copyright © 2017 by Merl Fennell
All rights reserved. No part of this book may be reproduced or transmitted in any form or by any means without written permission from the author.

ISBN 978-1-7324796-8-5

Printed in the United States of America

Publishing info: Fennell Adventures LLC
info@fennelladventures.com
678-895-7468

How to read this book:

This is **NOT** your ordinary read each page from start to finish! You will decide which order your Hawaiian adventure will go. All you have to do is choose between the pages in the color **RED.**
This way you can read this same book several times in a variety of ways!
Enjoy ! 🙂

Thank you from Jace

God, for sacrificing his son to save souls!
Jiyah, my older sister, for being a good sister!
Merl, my younger brother, for being the best lil' brother ever!
Dad, for the love you give to me! My mommy, Jennaye,
for supporting, loving, and showing me how to keep the faith!

"Do not worry about anything, but in everything by prayer and supplication with thanksgiving let your requests be made known to God.."
Bible verse:
Philippians 4:6 (NIV version)

Aloha, my friend! I am Jace Fennell your official tour guide! I am going to take you on an incredible adventure to the beautiful islands of Hawaii. You will join me and my family on a pretty cool vacation to ALL of the islands of Hawaii.

We will have tons of fun! We will eat delicious food, explore fun activities, experience the Polynesian culture, as well as learn many facts! We will create memories that will last us a lifetime....Let's Go!

WELCOME!

We live on the East Coast, so we will be taking an 11 hour flight to Hawaii. Let's make it fun by listening to some hip-hop music using our Beats by Dre. I have been on quite a few airplane rides, but it's always important to pray, so let's start.

"Dear God, Please see us through by wrapping your arms of safety around us tight. I know you will always be with us on any adventure that we take in life. Lord, we totally need you now, Amen."

This is an AWESOME adventure book, where YOU decide how the story goes, so choose wisely. Once we land, tell me exactly where you would like to explore first.

If you are adventurous, let's have fun on page 5.

If you are ready to shop, let's start spending on page 12.

If you are a city child like me, climbing a crater in Honolulu will be a new adventure for you too! OK, we have just arrived at Diamond Head Crater. I think my brother, Merl may be too young to climb with us, but we will let him join us anyway!

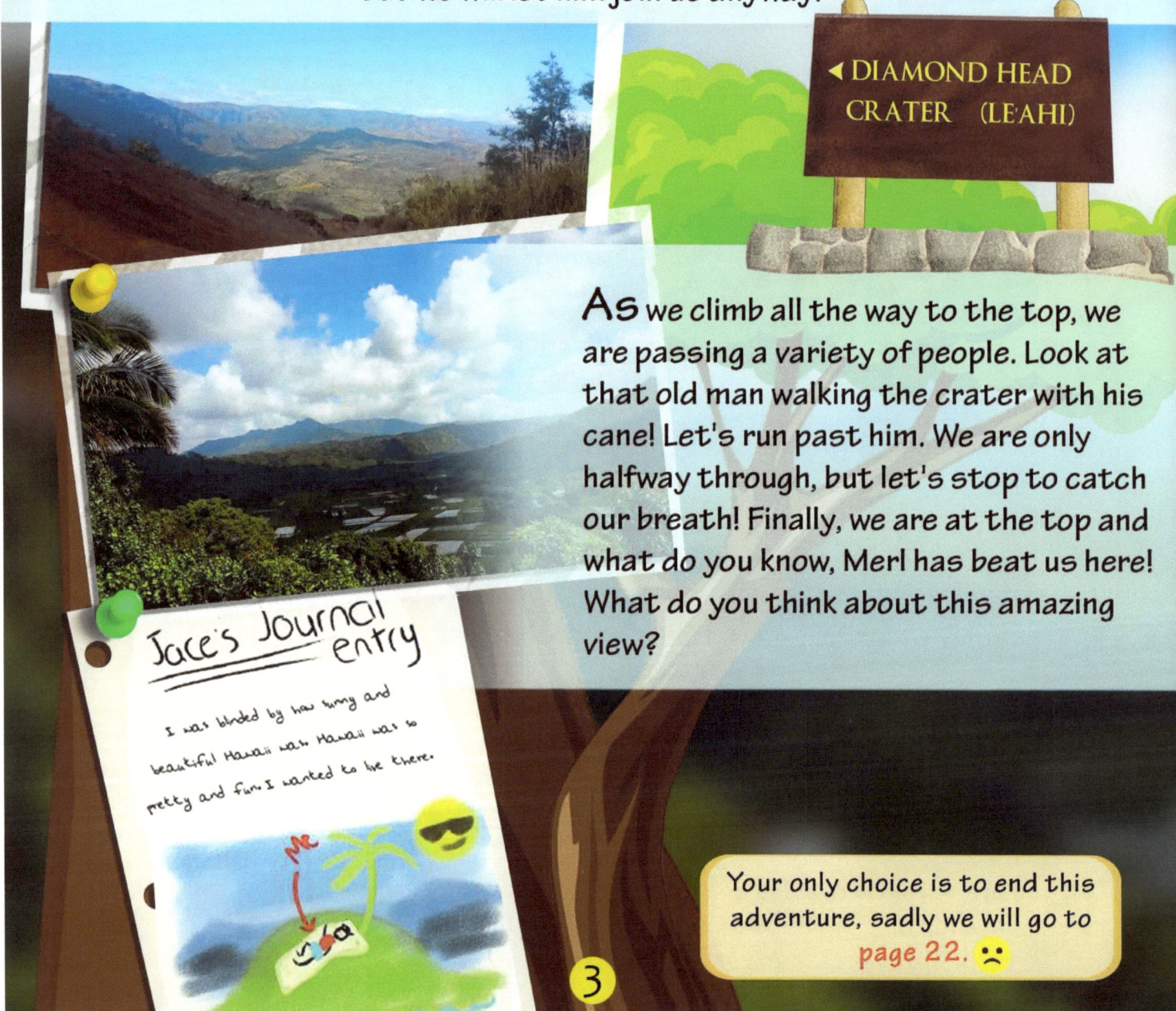

◀ DIAMOND HEAD CRATER (LEAHI)

As we climb all the way to the top, we are passing a variety of people. Look at that old man walking the crater with his cane! Let's run past him. We are only halfway through, but let's stop to catch our breath! Finally, we are at the top and what do you know, Merl has beat us here! What do you think about this amazing view?

Jace's Journal entry

I was blinded by how sunny and beautiful Hawaii was. Hawaii was so pretty and fun. I wanted to live there.

Your only choice is to end this adventure, sadly we will go to **page 22.** ☹

A great way to explore the Polynesian culture is at a Luau. Please grab a shirt or dress covered with flowers so we can fit right in with the natives. As we enter the Luau, we are being welcomed with a lei to wear around our neck or head. Let's join my siblings and the other children that are playing the Hawaiian games. If we look behind us, a real pig is roasting on an open fire. Our food selection is salmon, pork, papaya, pineapples, rice and veggies.

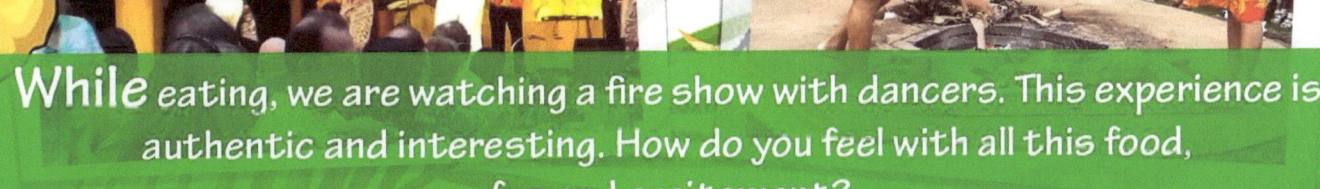

While eating, we are watching a fire show with dancers. This experience is authentic and interesting. How do you feel with all this food, fun and excitement?

If you would like to board the cruise, let's go to page 6.

If you would like to see an incredible waterfall, let's go to page 7.

Did you know that there is a Wet N Wild in Honolulu? In total, they have 25 water rides that are super fun! Let's go on my favorite ride, The Raging River. We will sit in this tube with my family.

Be careful as we get in! Hold on tight!
Close your eyes and scream as we go very fast!

Weeeeeeeee!

If you would like to experience the Polynesian culture, let's go to page 4.

If you would like to check out the hotel, let's go to page 9.

We did a pre-vacation at Honolulu, but now we will board the Norwegian Pride Cruise Ship to explore more islands. Other islands that we will explore are Maui, Kauai, and the Big Island including Hilo and Kona. Look how huge this boat is! It has several restaurants, shows and activities. Of course, we will hit the pool first! I also think we will have lots of fun in the kids' camp. I bet we will meet lots of kids! We even have an opportunity to perform in the kid talent show. Which talent will you share in the talent show?

If you would like to climb a crater, let's go to page 3.

If you would like to end this adventure, let's go to page 22.

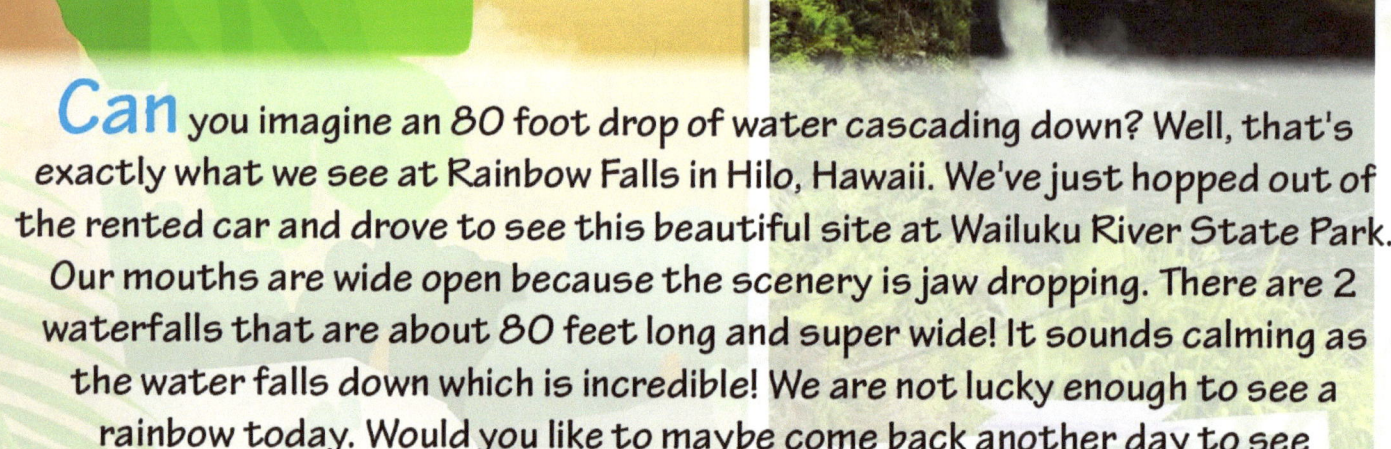

Can you imagine an 80 foot drop of water cascading down? Well, that's exactly what we see at Rainbow Falls in Hilo, Hawaii. We've just hopped out of the rented car and drove to see this beautiful site at Wailuku River State Park. Our mouths are wide open because the scenery is jaw dropping. There are 2 waterfalls that are about 80 feet long and super wide! It sounds calming as the water falls down which is incredible! We are not lucky enough to see a rainbow today. Would you like to maybe come back another day to see if we are able to see a rainbow?

If you would like to go eat and learn about pineapples, let's go to page 18.

If you would like to end this adventure, let's go to page 22.

I believe the best shaved ice can be found in Kona at Scandinavian Shave Ice! Shaved ice is similar to water ice, Italian ice, or a snow cane, but it is a lot better than all of them combined.

We are inside of the shop and have a huge selection to pick from. We can choose from over 60 flavors such as Bubble gum or Passion Fruit. We can even choose toppings like snow cap (condensed milk) or gummy bears. Of course, we are ordering delectable Mango with snow cap on top. Which flavor are you picking? This treat just made our day!

If you would like to go to the Disney Resort, let's go to page 19.

If you would like to learn about the past, let's go to page 20.

We are staying at the military hotel, Hale Koa. Look at this open entrance! It's very nice. There is a swimming pool, and in just a few steps we can walk to the beach. I bet you are pretty tired since there is a 5-hour time difference from the east coast to Hawaii. The hotel is a great place to get some rest.

If you would like to see the surfers and the tortoises", let's go to page 16.

If you would like to grab a bite to eat, let's go to page 17.

From our cruise ship, we were able to see breath taking views of all the Na Pali Coast. It is a shoreline of beautiful mountains and rainbows. Look at the colors, they are majestic and calming. The entire boat is looking from every open space at this amazing view. There are not many other views that could compare to this.

If you would like to grab a snack, let's go to page 10.

If you would like to go on a road trip adventure, let's go to page 21.

One of the shopping malls, we are walking through right now is Ala Moana. It is the world's largest open air mall. Even though we are shopping, the sky is above our head.

They have **290 stores** to shop inside. While we shop, we can experience the Polynesian culture with live music and hula dancers. My sister Jiyah is purchasing flip flops and creating her own design. You may want to do the same for yourself or a family member.

If you would like to experience the Polynesian culture, let's go to page 4.

If you would like to get some shaved ice, let's go to page 8.

On the Big Island, we went down under in a submarine. The tour was by Atlantis Adventures. First, you take a small ferry boat to the submarine. Once you get to the submarine, you have to step down into it. Each person has a seat with a circle port window to look through. They will give you a guide with fish labeled for you to search for. It was really exciting to actually find fish from the guide. I found several Unicorn fish.

Did you also see the other fishes and whales?

If you would like to learn about the past, let's go to page 20.

If you would like to end this adventure, let's go to page 22.

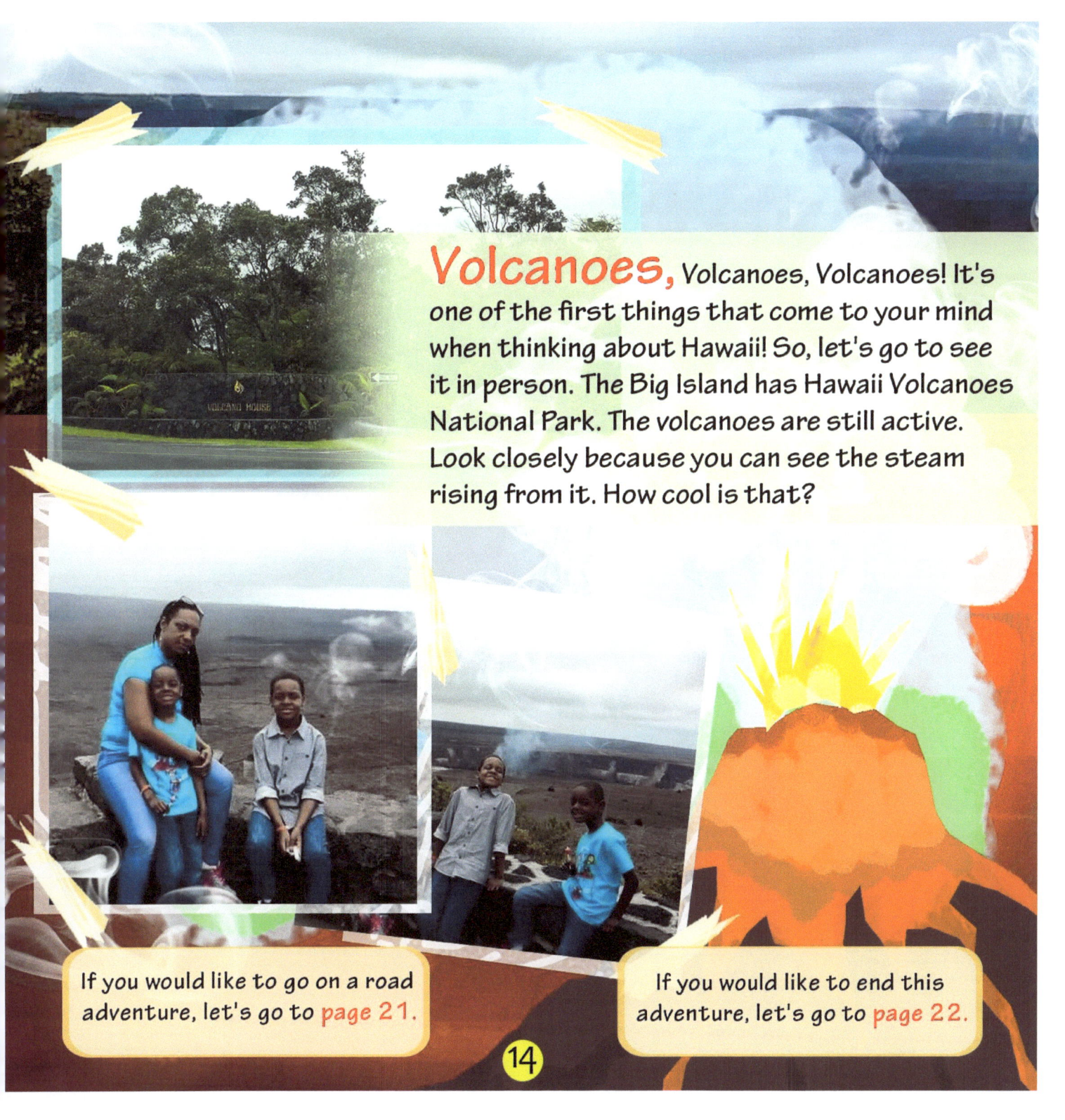

Volcanoes, Volcanoes, Volcanoes! It's one of the first things that come to your mind when thinking about Hawaii! So, let's go to see it in person. The Big Island has Hawaii Volcanoes National Park. The volcanoes are still active. Look closely because you can see the steam rising from it. How cool is that?

If you would like to go on a road adventure, let's go to page 21.

If you would like to end this adventure, let's go to page 22.

Of all the islands, Kauai by far is the best! Look around at the beautiful water and beautiful trees! I like this island the best because it is what I pictured Hawaii to be like. It has tropical trees and a beach with clear water. My sister, brother, you and I are being buried in the sand. Next, we will go on the boogie board given to us by another family. We will have to be extra careful in the deep water! These awesome memories in Hawaii will last us a lifetime!

If you would like to go to a Luau, let's go to page 4.

If you would like to learn about the past, let's go to page 20.

One of the most adventurous activities to see or try in Hawaii is surfing. On our way to Road to Hana, we were able to stop at a body of water. At this body of water were a group of surfers. They were riding huge waves and it was an incredible site to see. These guys were riding waves and it looked so easy because they were not falling off. I wanted to try to surf so bad once I saw them.

We also were able to see huge tortoises just lying at the base of the water in the sand. I thought this was cool too!

If you would like to go on an underwater adventure, let's go to page 13.

If you would like to go to the beach on a beautiful island, let's go to page 15.

The high arc of the M is posted across the United States and can be seen from a far. We stopped at McDonald's to grab a bite to eat. The breakfast menu is expanded to include the Polynesian culture. Can you guess which added items they serve? Yes, rice and spam! Since I was in Hawaii, I had to try it.

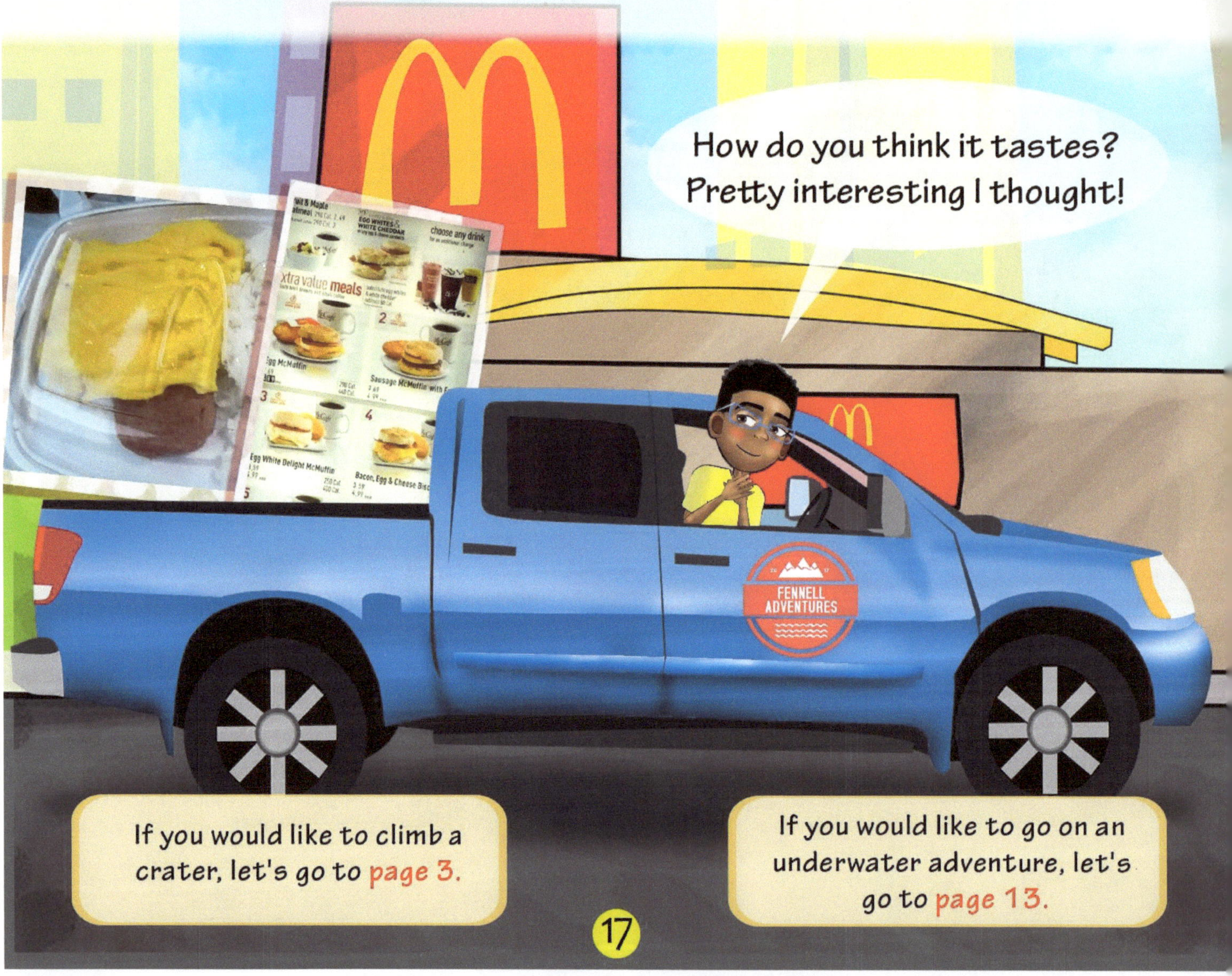
How do you think it tastes? Pretty interesting I thought!
FENNELL ADVENTURES

If you would like to climb a crater, let's go to page 3.

If you would like to go on an underwater adventure, let's go to page 13.

Pineapples are a great sweet treat! Now, we are at the Dole Pineapple Plantation near Honolulu. Here you can find out many facts about pineapples such as the length of time they grow. It takes about 20 months for the plant to produce a pineapple from the ground. I think that is a loooong time. While at the plantation, we are touring the fields by train, going through a crazy maze, seeing beautiful gardens, and eating freshly grown pineapples covered with ice cream! One of the best treats here is a pineapple float. Let's enjoy one together? The mixture of flavors is very delicious!

If you would like to grab a snack, let's go to page 10.

If you would like to end this adventure, let's go to page 22.

My family and i looooove...

Disney

We have been there many times, so it was a must to see the Hawaiian Disney Resort. Aulani is what it is called, but they do not have rides. You can stay on site and enjoy the beach, water activities, or eat delicious food. We were there just to eat at the restaurant and explore the free lagoon. The food was excellent and included the famous fresh POG juice, exotic fruits, and red velvet pancakes. As we ate the view was cool! Look to your left!

If you would like to see an incredible view of the coastline, let's go to page 11.

If you would like to eat and learn about pineapples, let's go to page 18.

An historic event to learn about in Hawaii is Pearl Harbor. On December 7, 1941, Pearl Harbor was a surprise attack by the Japanese Armed Forces that started WWII. We are arriving early because only a certain amount of visitors are allowed in daily. Once we go in we will watch a video of the event. Then we can purchase our earphones to get a narrated tour. The audio tour is well worth the money because it explains the event in full detail. There is a ferry that we are taking to see the Arizona Memorial. This is where a list is compiled of soldiers who lost their lives during the war. If we look closely in the water, we can still see oil from the actual event.

If you would like to see an incredible view of the coastline, let's go to page 11.

If you would like to learn and see an active volcano, let's go to page 14.

Now the Road to Hana is an adventure all by itself! It is a winding road in Maui that elevates extremely high allowing the site of amazing views! It actually feels like a real life roller coaster. Since we are brave enough to drive it, we are seeing incredible views and black sand beaches. We have to pull over because we are getting dizzy just riding in the car. Along the way, we will stop at a food truck to eat delicious hamburgers. Although we did not make it all the way through, we are still able to see the black sand beach. My mom and sister even purchased a shirt that says, "I survived the Road to Hana!" Maybe we can purchase a shirt, too!

If you would like to board the cruise, let's go to page 6.

If you would like to end this adventure, let's go to page 22.

Thank you for allowing me to take you on such a memorable adventure of Hawaii with my family. I hope you enjoyed the adventure that you chose! I hope that you will read again and again to create more awesome adventures.

Always remember that God is with you on this adventure called life. The journey will be what you make it. I wish peace and blessings in your life! I hope to see you in my next destination adventure book!

Start another Hawaiian adventure from the beginning!

Hawaiian Excursion Guide:
Please take this book with you to Hawaii and check each box as you visit.

- ☐ Aulani
- ☐ Surfers
- ☐ Wet N Wild
- ☐ Kauai Beach
- ☐ McDonald's
- ☐ Pearl Harbor
- ☐ Road to Hana
- ☐ Na Pali Coast
- ☐ Rainbow Falls
- ☐ Polynesian Luau
- ☐ Hotel (Hale Koa)
- ☐ Atlantis Adventures
- ☐ Diamond Head Crater
- ☐ Norwegian Cruise Ship
- ☐ Scandinavian Shave Ice
- ☐ Dole Pineapple Plantation
- ☐ Ala Moana Shopping Mall
- ☐ Hawaii Volcano National Park
- ☐ Mauna Loa Macadamia Nut Factory